My Hero's Journey:
From Struggle to Strength

A Post-Traumatic Growth Tale

Daniel Navarro Jr.

First Edition
Published by
Strive To Thrive LLC

Cover and interior design by Daniel Navarro Jr.

To my wife,
thank you for choosing me and for walking beside me on this journey
called life. I love you.

And to my boys,
I hope this book serves as a compass, guiding you as you find your own
way.

Preface

This book is a collection of moments, snapshots of a life shaped by experience, challenge, and growth.

It is, in many ways, a time capsule.

A reflection of who I was, who I am, and who I continue to become.

There was a time when I didn't fully understand the significance of my story.

Like many people, I lived through experiences without always stopping to process them. Some moments I carried with pride. Others I buried, avoided, or simply moved past.

But over time, I began to realize something important:

Every experience leaves something behind.

A lesson.
A perspective.
A piece of wisdom.

This book is my way of capturing those pieces.

Not as a finished product, but as a living reflection of my journey through life and Post-Traumatic Growth.

The stories within these pages are real.

They are based on my experiences, moments of service, loss, reflection, and discovery. Some are difficult. Some are uplifting. All of them have shaped the way I see the world today.

Over the past years, I have learned that growth does not come from avoiding hardship.

It comes from facing it.

From understanding it.

From allowing it to teach us something about ourselves.

This book is not meant to provide all the answers.

It is not a guide to perfection.

It is an invitation.

An invitation to reflect on your own life.

To look at your own experiences, past and present, and consider what they may be teaching you.

To recognize that even in the most difficult moments, there is the potential for growth.

If one story in this book resonates with you,

If one moment causes you to pause and reflect,

If one idea helps you see your own journey a little differently,

Then this book has served its purpose.

Because at the end of the day, this is not just my story.

It is a reminder that we are all on a journey.

And within each of us,

There is more being written.

Daniel Navarro Jr.

The Journey

The Ordinary World
Chapter 1: A Beginning - Pg. 13

⌛

The Call to Adventure
Chapter 2: The Call - Pg. 17

⌛

Crossing the Threshold
Chapter 3: The Storm - Pg. 23

⌛

The Road of Trials
Chapter 4: The Unknown - Pg. 29

⌛

Tests, Allies, and Growth
Chapter 5: Lessons of Growth - Pg. 35

⌛

The Tests Deepen
Chapter 6: The Tests - Pg. 43

⌛

Approach to the Inner Cave
Chapter 7: The Cave - Pg. 51

⌛

The Ordeal
Chapter 8: The Dragon Pg. 59

⌛

The Reward (The Elixir)
Chapter 9: The Elixir - Pg. 69

⌛

The Return with the Gift
Chapter 10: A New Beginning: Living My Calling - Pg. 79

⌛

Reflection in Songs - Pg. 87

⌛

Acknowledgments & Influences - Pg. 95

Introduction

These chapters are reflection of a journey, one shaped by struggle, growth, and transformation.

It is not a story of perfection.
It is a story of becoming.

For many years, I lived a life defined by structure, purpose, and service.

The military gave me direction, identity, and a mission greater than myself.

But when that chapter of my life came to an end, I found myself stepping into something unfamiliar.

The unknown.

What followed was not a straight path.

It was filled with uncertainty, internal conflict, loss, and moments where I questioned who I was and where I was going.

But within those moments, something else began to take shape.

Growth.

Not the kind of growth that comes easily, but the kind that is formed through adversity.

The kind that challenges your beliefs, your identity, and your understanding of life itself.

This is what is known as Post-Traumatic Growth.

This book is my story of that growth.

Through storms, caves, tests, and moments of clarity, I began to understand that the experiences I once saw as setbacks were actually shaping me into something more.

This journey taught me the difference between surviving and thriving.

Between control and connection.

Between carrying everything, and learning what to release.

Most importantly, it taught me that growth is not a destination.

It is a daily practice.

As you read through these chapters, my hope is not that you see my story as something separate from your own, but that you find pieces of yourself within it.

Because no matter what you've been through.

You are not broken.

You are becoming.

Chapter 1
(A Beginning)

On January 1, 2019, I officially became a military retiree after 23 years of service. There is no doubt in my mind that the military shaped who I was at that time.

A year before my retirement, my wife and I had many conversations about what life would look like after completing 22 years of service. We weighed the pros and cons of stepping away. Eventually, we made the decision to move forward with retirement, but as that decision became real, so did the weight of it.

The organization that had supported us in every way would soon be behind us.

Still, it wasn't until about six months before retiring that the stress truly began to surface. It slowly worked its way into my thoughts, my emotions, and my sense of identity.

To understand this transition, it's important to recognize something many people don't see.

When a service member leaves the military, they aren't just changing jobs. They are stepping away from a way of life. A structure. A community. A shared purpose. For many, it's all they've known since leaving high school.

Walking away from that takes more than planning; it takes courage.

What I didn't realize at the time was that this was the beginning of my hero's journey.

In the years that followed, I found myself moving from one job to another, customer service, manufacturing supervisor, and project manager. On paper, it looked like progress.

But internally, something was off.

I couldn't quite put my finger on it, but I felt like something was missing.

As time went on, the stress began to build, personally, professionally, and mentally. My sense of direction started to fade, and I began blaming my state of mind on what I no longer had.

What I missed most was the sense of community, the camaraderie I had in the military.

I often described it like this:

It felt like I had been on a cruise ship with the people I served alongside and one day, without warning, I was dropped off alone on a large island, surrounded by a jungle in the middle of the ocean.

The days at work felt longer. The silence felt louder.

I felt alone.

There was also an internal conflict I couldn't yet see clearly.

One part of me wanted to climb the ladder of success, build a career, achieve more, and keep pushing forward.

Another part of me wanted something different, freedom, meaning, and a deeper sense of purpose.

At the time, I couldn't articulate it. I just knew something wasn't aligned.

I wasn't congruent.

My life didn't look the way I had imagined it would, and for the first time in a long time, I didn't have a clear structure to guide me.

In the study of Post-Traumatic Growth, developed by Richard Tedeschi, PhD and Lawrence Calhoun, PhD from the University of North Carolina at Charlotte, there is a concept often described as a "wellness triangle", encompassing the mind, body, finances, and spirit.

I won't go too deep into it here, but I want to share how I experienced these areas while in the military.

As a Non-Commissioned Officer in the United States Army, these elements were built into my daily life, whether I realized it or not.

The Mind:
I served in leadership roles where I coached, trained, and mentored others. I was constantly learning, teaching, and developing a mindset focused on growth and performance.

The Body:
Physical training wasn't optional; it was required. Being physically prepared was part of the mission.

The Finances:
The military provided stability, a steady income, structure, and resources to support both service members and their families.

The Spirit:
There was a clear sense of purpose, serving something greater than myself.

Looking back, I can now see that these areas were being supported for me without my awareness.

It was a blind spot.

I didn't realize how much structure I was operating within, until it was gone.

And that wasn't the only blind spot in my life.

Everything changed on April 16, 2022.

Chapter 2
(The Call)

As I mentioned earlier, my stress continued to build.

At the time, however, my mindset was focused on service, serving others outside of my occupation. I began sharing information on social media about programs that supported veterans who were struggling, all while being completely unaware of my own internal struggle.

I was advocating for others but not for myself.

While posting about these support programs, a mentor of mine reached out and asked if I would be interested in attending something called the Warrior PATHH Program, a peer-to-peer training experience designed to help veterans and first responders transform trauma into lifelong growth.

At the time, still blind to my own struggles, I told him no.

"I'm not struggling," I said. "I don't want to take a seat from someone who really needs it."

Looking back now, I often ask myself: What does "truly struggling" even mean?

Because the truth is, I was struggling. I just didn't recognize it.

A few months passed, and I continued pushing hard on social media, advocating for veteran support programs.

Eventually, I had another conversation with my mentor. I don't remember exactly how we circled back to the topic of me attending the program, but I do remember one thing clearly; he mentioned that it was also a leadership course.

At the time, I was heavily focused on being a servant leader in the online community.

That was enough for me.

I agreed to attend.

But not because I believed I needed help.

I went because I wanted to gain knowledge, so I could give it away to others.

It was still rooted in selfless service.

On April 8, 2022, I walked through the doors of the program.

I had no idea what was about to happen.

In the spirit of respect for the program and those who attend it, I won't go into specific details about what takes place. Instead, I'll share what I gained from the experience.

Because that's what matters most.

On the second day, something shifted.

The glass shattered.

I went in with the intention of taking notes to help others, but suddenly, my focus turned inward.

For the first time in a long time, I was paying attention to myself.

It was a shift from selflessness to what I now understand as necessary for selfishness, especially when it comes to self-care.

I realized something that had been true for years:

I had always put others before myself.

In the military, we're taught that leaders eat last. It's a principle grounded in service, responsibility, and care for others. It becomes part of who you are.

But what I didn't realize was that I had carried that mindset into every part of my life, even when it was no longer serving me.

So, I began asking myself:

When was I going to start taking care of myself?

Why had I never truly considered it before?

Maybe someone had said it to me along the way.

Maybe I wasn't ready to hear it.

But at that moment, I was listening.

And that's what mattered.

Another lesson that stayed with me was the importance of being present.

As my mentor would say, "Be where your feet are."

Not in the past.
Not in the future.
But fully in the moment you are standing in.

That kind of presence changes everything.

It allows you to notice what you would normally overlook, to truly see people, experiences, and even the small details of life.

I remember one moment that captured this perfectly.

I was standing with a friend, and we found ourselves watching a group of ants moving along the ground at our feet.

At first, it seemed like nothing.

But as we paid attention, we noticed something interesting. The group would occasionally pause, and a couple of ants would move ahead, almost like they were conducting reconnaissance before the rest continued forward.

It reminded me of military tactics.

Later, I learned that ants aren't conducting reconnaissance in the way we understand it. They're following pheromone trails, with certain ants encountering obstacles and adjusting the path for the group.

But that wasn't the point.

The point was, we were present.

And because we were present, we were able to witness something we would have otherwise missed.

That week gave me more than knowledge.

It gave me a perspective.

It introduced me to a different way of living, one rooted in awareness, self-care, and intentional growth.

For the first time in a long time, I felt like I had stepped away from the noise of life.

I took a knee, not out of exhaustion, but out of intention.

And I began to ask myself:

When was the last time I truly allowed myself to pause?
To be still?
To just be?

I could probably count those moments using only one hand.

That week changed that.

It was a profound experience, one that set me on a path I am still walking today.

But as I would soon learn.

Life was waiting on the other side of those doors.

And it was about to test everything I had just begun to understand.

Chapter 3
(A Storm)

On the evening of July 16, 2022, I joined six friends for a 30-minute pontoon ride across the lake to catch some live music.

The night began calm and simple, but as we reached the far shore, dark clouds gathered. Calls from the campsite confirmed what we already sensed; the storm had arrived. With no rain gear, only towels, we made the choice to head back, knowing we were about to be soaked.

As we pushed off, the water began to churn beneath us.

The moon and stars disappeared behind heavy clouds, replaced only by flashes of lightning tearing across the lake ahead. Anxiety settled in.

What started as a light spray quickly turned into a furious downpour. Rain came down like bullets, pounding us without mercy from the front of the boat. It felt like the scene from Forrest Gump, when Lt. Dan is yelling at the storm, daring it to do its worst.

At the front of the boat, the captain took the brunt of it, no windshield, no shelter, only grit. The rain drops pounced all over him, as he showed no fear to the lighting and thunder.

It looked as though the storm was throwing everything it had at him, daring him to turn back. But he never faltered. Like a seasoned warrior, he pressed on as if yelling back,

"Is that all you've got?"

The closer we came to camp, the fiercer the rain grew. Spirits dropped as everyone braced against the storm.

And then, it happened.

From the darkness came a voice.

Small. Clear. Steady.

The youngest among us, just 11 years old, began to sing.

At first, it was a soft melody cutting through the chaos like a beam of light. Then it spread. One by one, we joined in, singing Hakuna Matata, and also belting out Don McLain's American Pie.

Laughter followed.

And just like that, the storm didn't feel like an enemy anymore. It became part of the memory we created.

What started as a miserable ride turned into something meaningful.

We were still soaked, but we weren't defeated.

We were united.

And it all began with the voice of a child, reminding us that joy can outshine fear, even in the darkest storm.

This was one of my first trips after completing Warrior PATHH, alongside one of my brothers from the program. His daughter changed the entire tone of that night.

Looking back, that moment became a metaphor for my life.

Because while that storm lasted an hour.

The storms in my life were still being built.

After Warrior PATHH, work life continued to bring pressure, problems, decisions, and stress as a project manager.

I had learned valuable lessons, but I hadn't yet built the habits to support them. I hadn't created boundaries. My mind remained consumed with work, making it difficult to stay consistent with the practices I had been introduced to.

I knew effort and attitude were essential.

But knowing something and living it are two different things.

This was going to require action, and consistent effort on my part.

There was also something missing.

Something I now know was critical to my growth.

I wasn't using my support system as I should have, my "3 to 5." The people who would hold me accountable, support me, and keep me aligned with the path I was trying to walk.

As time went on, the pressure continued to build.

And then life delivered a moment that changed everything.

An important person in my life passed away, my mother-in-law.

Growing up, I had heard all the stereotypes about mother-in-laws. But she was the complete opposite.

During my time in the military, when I was gone for months, and in some cases a year, she was always there.

She supported my family.

She supported me.

She was someone I could talk to when things got difficult.

She wasn't just my mother-in-law.

She was my best friend.

When she passed away on May 25, 2023, Memorial Day, from an unexpected medical issue, it sent me into a whirlwind of emotions.

She was the first person in my personal life that I had ever lost.

And she wasn't just family; she was the foundation of it.

At the time, I didn't fully understand how much her loss was impacting me.

It wasn't until years later, looking back, that I began to see it clearly.

During that period, I was also attending graduate school.

Within a year, I failed multiple classes, to the point that I stepped away from the program entirely for two years.

And at the time, I didn't know if I would ever return.

In that season of my life, I had lost more than just a person.

I had lost a sense of stability.

A sense of connection.

A sense of direction.

I was searching for answers.

I had been given knowledge, practice, and exercises for self-care, but I hadn't yet fully implemented them into my life.

Once again, a guide appeared; an expert companion.

A friend reached out, offering support, direction, and a light in the darkness.

He helped me to understood something important:

Hope was not an action plan.

And action was required.

Through reflection, I began to reconnect with something I had always known:

My purpose was never about things.

It was about people.

For years, I had served my country, a higher calling, a mission beyond myself.

And now I realized.

I still wanted to serve.

But I also needed to learn how to serve myself first.

Through long walks in nature and conversations with my wife, I made a decision.

One I never would have made before Warrior PATHH.

I chose to quit my job.
No backup plan.
No safety net.

Before, I would have called that irresponsible.

But this time, it felt necessary.

I stopped running toward success.

And started moving toward purpose.

That decision marked the beginning of a new chapter in my life.

The moment I shifted.

From working.

To serving.

Chapter 4
(Into the Unknown)

On June 27, 2023, I submitted my two-week resignation.

For the first time since high school, I had no job.

Two weeks after graduating, I was on a bus headed for basic training. Back then, I had a clear path, purpose, occupation, a destination.

This time was different.

This time, I was stepping into the unknown.

It felt like my first true step into what Joseph Campbell describes as The Hero's Journey, leaving behind what is familiar and venturing into uncertainty.

The day I walked away from what I once called normal. I didn't know what was ahead of me.

But I did know one thing:

I wasn't walking alone.

Along the way, I met mentors and guides, people who had already begun shaping the path in front of me.

To be clear, I didn't stop moving forward after leaving my job.

I simply changed direction.

I began volunteering at a non-profit organization called The Big Red Barn Retreat, which was the same place where I had attended the Warrior PATHH Program.

What started as volunteering became something much deeper.

I had shifted.

From working, to serving.

For months, I showed up.

Helping where I could. Supporting the mission. Preparing for incoming students. Doing the behind-the-scenes work that often goes unseen.

And then, after three months, an opportunity presented itself.

I was invited to become part of the organization.

The feeling was something I hadn't experienced in a long time.

Purpose.

Not assigned but chosen.

I felt that same calling I once had in the military, the opportunity to serve something greater than myself.

And to this day, I still serve there.

People often ask me if I work at the organization.

My answer has never changed:

"I don't work there, I serve there."

And that's not just a choice of words.

It's a mindset.

On some Fridays, I host a group conversation called Gather for Growth.

Each session is an opportunity to connect, listen, and grow together.

And every time I step into that space, I am reminded:
It is an honor to be there for those who are seeking guidance.

While serving others, something else began to happen.
I was also healing.

For the first time, I had a community around me, people who supported me, challenged me, and helped guide me through decisions in my life.

Because of that support, I began to respond instead of react.
I was no longer facing challenges alone.

The stories shared within that space, the vulnerability, the honesty, the courage, it all reminded me of something important:

I wasn't the only one navigating storms.

And in hearing their stories, I found strength to face my own.

Over time, I began to see something differently.

This place I was serving.

It wasn't just a location.

It was a space for transformation.

A place many might hesitate to enter, but one that held something valuable on the other side.

It was the cave.

The very cave we fear to enter.

The one that holds the treasure we seek.

One day, during a nature walk, I shared my story with a participant, how I had quit my job without a plan, stepping fully into uncertainty.

He paused and asked me:

"Do you realize what you did?"

At the time, I didn't.

I shrugged it off.

But he didn't.

He spoke about the courage it took to make a decision like that.

To walk away from stability, without knowing what would come next.

Later that day, I reflected on his words.

And for the first time, I began to understand the weight of that decision.

Because if I hadn't taken that step,

There's a good chance I wouldn't be where I am now.

Serving others.

Living with purpose.

Walking a path aligned with who I truly am.

Every storm has a rainbow.

But it's the choices we make within the storm that creates the possibility of seeing it.

In Chapter 1, I described feeling like I had been dropped off on an island, alone, surrounded by a jungle, unsure of where to go.

But over time, I realized something important:

I had walked into that jungle.

And when I did, I found others.

I was never truly alone.

I had just been choosing to stay on the shoreline.

Looking back.

Holding on.

Living in the past.

As I began to move forward, my circle grew.

What once was a search for three to five people became something much greater.

A network.
A community.
A support system.

And as I continued to share my story, openly and honestly, I began to uncover parts of myself I hadn't yet explored.

New spaces.
New truths.
New layers.
New caves.

Some of those caves, I thought I would have faced much earlier in my journey.

But life has its own timing.

And one of those caves.

Was waiting for me.

It was the cave of my childhood; one I would come to understand more deeply later in this journey.

Chapter 5
(Lessons of Growth)

A year had passed since I was given the opportunity to serve again.

During that time, I found myself in a season of exploration, leaning into my wellness practices and beginning to understand myself on a deeper level.

One concept, in particular, stood out to me:

The difference between connection and control.

Connection is about understanding, presence, and shared experiences.

It is built on trust and openness. It allows people to feel seen, heard, and valued.

It says: "I'm here with you."

Control, on the other hand, is about managing outcomes, behaviors, and situations.

It is often driven by fear, uncertainty, or urgency. It shows up in the need to fix, direct, or correct others.

It says: "I need this to go my way."

This realization hit me hard.

Because for many years, I had been operating from a place of control.

I would use language like:

"You need to do this."
"Do it this way."
"You're doing it wrong."

As I reflected on it, a simple thought came to mind:

If we could truly control others, then someone would be controlling me.

And that's not something any of us would want.

So, the question became:

How did I get here?

That's when I had another realization.

After spending so many years in the military, I had been conditioned through repetition to operate from a place of control.

It wasn't who I was.

It was what I had learned to do.

As a sergeant in the Army, I had thousands of repetitions telling people what to do, how to do it, and when to do it.

Over time, it became automatic.

It reminded me of training at the firing range.

We would conduct repetition drills, raising our weapon, switching from safe to semi, engaging the target, and then placing the weapon back on safe before lowering it.

We did it so many times that eventually, we didn't have to think about it.

It just happened.

That's how my mindset had become.

Control had become automatic.

And that led me to another question:

What else was I doing on autopilot that was affecting my relationships?

That question sparked curiosity within me.
A desire to explore areas of my life that needed growth and change.

One of those areas was my relationship with my wife.

Over the years, through deployments, long hours, and the demands of work, we had grown apart.

For a long time, I told myself that was the reason.

But the truth was harder to accept.

I had contributed to that distance.

I hadn't sought help.

I hadn't educated myself on how to manage stress in a healthy way.

And the control mindset I carried didn't stay at work, it came home with me.

As a child, I made a promise to myself that I would never hurt my wife physically, based on what I experienced growing up, a story I will share later.

But what I didn't realize was this:

I was still causing harm.

Not physically.

But emotionally.

Through absence.
Through disconnection.

Through a lack of presence.

That realization was difficult, but necessary.

Around that time, I asked a peer if she had any advice on building a stronger relationship.

She asked me if I had ever heard of the book *The 5 Love Languages* by Gary Chapman.

I told her I hadn't, but I would look into it.

A few weeks later, I was having dinner with a friend and his son.

During our conversation about relationships, his son, who was about my age, asked me the same question:

"Have you ever read *The 5 Love Languages*?"

That got my attention.

Then it happened a third time.

And this time, it hit differently.

One day, I was looking for a pair of scissors at home. My wife told me to check inside the bench in the kitchen nook.

As I searched, I came across old letters from my time deployed in the military.

I picked them up.

And underneath them.

Was the book.

The 5 Love Languages.

When I saw it, a wave of emotion came over me.
Because I realized something:

At some point in our marriage, my wife bought that book, likely hoping it would help us connect.

And I had missed it.

That moment stayed with me.

But I also reminded myself of something important:

That was who I was then.

This is who I am now.

And now, I can do something about it.

I had learned not to live in the past, but to learn from it. To reflect, without residing.

That became a new theme in my life.

Not just a concept, but a lifestyle.

Because what I began to understand was this:

Post-Traumatic Growth isn't a temporary solution.

It's daily practice.

The more curious I became, the more I started to see life differently.

I began to believe something I hadn't fully understood before:

Life doesn't happen to us.

It happens for us.

Reflection in Song:

Waiting For A Light

I'm sitting here
In the dark
Waiting for a light,
Or a shooting star

Well, I'm sitting in the dark
Waiting for a light up
Waiting for a shooting star to
Light up the night

When I was young
The days where cold
The winds of change
Blew through my soul.

Everywhere
I looked around
All I saw were
Shadows on the walls

So, I grab my bags
and left on a trail
never looking back to
see what's there.

I'm sitting here
In the dark
Waiting for a light,
Or a shooting star

Well, I'm sitting in the dark
Waiting for a light up
Waiting for a shooting star to
Light up the night

I said
Heyy Yoo!
Heyy
Let the four winds blow

And I said,
Heyy Yoo!
Waiting for that
Heavenly glow

G-C-G-D
(Guitar Chords)

As the years have passed
The days are cold
The winds of change
Keep blowing through my soul.

Whren a door appears
Around some trees,
I'm walking in a labyrinth
With a warm cool breeze.

Then, I grab a rock from my
Heart of within
And I throw it in fire so
My life could begin

Well, I'm still sitting
In the dark
Waiting for a light,
Or a shooting star

I said
Heyy Yoo!
Heyy
Let the four winds blow

And I said,
Heyy Yoo!
Waiting for that
Heavenly glow

G-C-G-D
(Guitar Chords)

Now the winds of change
Begins to soar
My Gratitude for life runs
Through my soul

Now I'm looking back
from where I came
I get to write my story without
Any shame

Then I stand right up
With my head up high
As shower of shooting stars
Light up the sky

Well, I'm not sitting in the dark
Waiting for a light
Or waiting for a shooting star
light up the night.

No, I'm now standing up
With my head up high
As a shower of shooting stars
light up the sky.

I said
Heyy Yoo!
Heyy
Let the four winds blow

And I said,
Heyy Yoo!
Watching that
Heavenly glow

(Guitar Chords)

Chapter 6
(The Tests)

In this chapter, I want to share a few moments from my life, situations where I was given the opportunity to see where I truly was in my Post-Traumatic Growth journey.

Not in theory.

But in real life.

One Thursday afternoon, I was scheduled to pick up my 19-year-old son at 4:00 PM from school, which is about three miles from our house.

That same day, I was volunteering at an event scheduled from 1:00 PM to 3:00 PM.

But like many things in life, it ran longer than expected.

At some point, I glanced at my phone.

Multiple text messages.
Several missed calls.

From both my son and my wife.

It was 4:10 PM.

I was late, very late.

And with traffic, I knew it would take me at least 45 minutes to get there.

By the time I got home, it was 5:15 PM.

My wife didn't say much.

She didn't have to.

The silence said everything.

A few minutes later, my son walked in through the back door. He went straight to his room, clearly upset, and said he didn't want to talk about it.

So I didn't push.

I gave him space.

About an hour later, I heard him laughing in his room, playing on his PC with friends.

I walked in, kept it simple, and apologized.

"I'm sorry," I said.

He responded, "It's okay," in a tone that said it wasn't fully okay, but it was enough for now.

In the past, moments like this would have taken a different turn.

When I failed to follow through on something, I would isolate myself.

I would carry the weight of it.

I would replay it over and over.

And more often than not, I would cancel everything else in my life to try and "make up" for it.

The next day, I had a scheduled event.

Two years ago, I wouldn't have gone.

I would have stayed home, stuck in guilt, trying to fix something that had already happened.

But this time was different.

I was intentional.

I recognized what I was feeling, but I didn't let it control me. I had a choice:

Stay stuck in the past.

Or move forward with awareness.

I chose to move forward.

I gave myself grace.

From the moment I apologized to my son, I made a commitment:

I would not make a reactive decision.

I would stay present.

Because of that choice, something interesting happened. That same night, my son returned to himself, as if nothing had happened.

And the next morning, I was able to show up for a dear friend who had just lost a family member.

That moment reminded me:

Growth isn't about being perfect.

It's about responding differently.

Another moment came on a Saturday morning.

My wife and I were driving to a cat foster event with two of our foster cats.

As we were traveling on the interstate, I suddenly felt the car jolt.

The front right tire had gone flat.

I calmly turned on the hazard lights and carefully moved us to the shoulder.

I looked over at my wife and said,

"It's going to be alright."

We quickly made a plan.

I would change the tire.

We would call her father, who happened to live just five minutes away, and he would take her to the event.

Everything unfolded exactly as we discussed.

He arrived within 15 minutes.

I finished changing the tire.

They left for the event.

And I headed back home.

When I got home, I paused and reflected.
Because I knew something had changed.

In the past, that moment would have looked very different.

There would have been frustration.

Complaints.

Maybe even an argument.

But none of that happened.

I stayed calm.

I responded.

I didn't react.

That moment wasn't just about a flat tire.

It was a test.

A measure of where I was in my life.

And for the first time, I felt proud.

Not because the situation went perfectly,

But because I handled it differently.

I wasn't trying to control people.

I was managing myself.

Using the right mindset, at the right time, for the right situation.

That's growth.

Moments like these helped me understand something deeper:

Life doesn't happen to us.

It happens for us.

Each situation, big or small, became an opportunity.

An opportunity to check in.

To reflect.

To grow.

That doesn't mean I always get it right.

There have been times I've fallen short.

But now, instead of staying stuck in those moments.

I give myself grace.

And I keep moving forward.

Because I've learned this:

Challenges aren't obstacles.

They are invitations.

Invitations to grow into the person we are becoming.

Chapter 7
(The Cave)

My relationships at home began to improve based on what I had learned.

I became more present.

More aware.
More intentional.

And over time, that presence helped rebuild connections that had once been strained.

But even as things around me improved.

Something within me remained untouched.

There were still caves I hadn't entered.

Years had passed since attending Warrior PATHH, yet I had not fully faced the deeper parts of my story, the experiences that shaped me into who I had become.

In the early stages of my post-traumatic growth journey, my focus was on rebuilding relationships.

And that mattered.

It still does.

But now, two and a half years later, I found myself ready to explore places within me that I wasn't ready to face before.

In this chapter, and the next, I will share two traumatic experiences that impacted my life.

I will do so with respect for those involved, without going into unnecessary detail.

Because this isn't about reliving the moment.

It's about understanding its impact.

On July 23, 2013, during a combat deployment in Afghanistan, our platoon was conducting dismounted operations in a village near our combat outpost.

As the platoon sergeant, I positioned myself at the exit point of the village.

My responsibility was to ensure accountability, to count every soldier out and maintain proper spacing as we moved.

Then it happened.

As the last soldier passed me and only a few minutes had gone by, a large explosion erupted in the middle of the platoon.

I saw it.

I heard it.

And in that moment, everything changed.

Debris and fragments cut through the air.

Later, I would realize what I heard passing my ears were ball bearings.

Instinct took over.

My medic and I moved immediately to assess casualties.

We called in a 9-line MEDEVAC and requested a quick reaction force.

I reported status, established security, and stayed focused on the mission.

Minutes later, the QRF arrived.

The first person on scene was my First Sergeant.

What I share next is not to discredit him, but to provide context for the moment.

Because in combat, what needs to happen, happens.

He looked me directly in the eyes. And he saw it.

He saw me on the edge.

And he said:

"Don't you do it. You suck it in and help me get your brother through this."

In that moment, I picked up what I now call a resiliency rock.

I compartmentalized everything I was feeling.

And I responded:

"Roger that."

We evacuated our Heroes and wounded.

Completed the necessary assessments.

And returned to base.

Mission complete.

But something came back with me.

That rock.

And for years, I carried it.

Without knowing how to put it down.

The military trained me to be resilient.

To move forward.

To accomplish the mission, no matter what.

But what I didn't learn,

Was how to move forward from it.

Yes, I sat down with professionals.

Yes, I talked about that day.

But talking about it was easy, because part of me never left it.

I was still there.

The idea was that the more we talked about it, the more we could let it go.

But something inside me resisted.

I didn't want to go back there.

I could feel it.

And even though the support came from a place of care, I wasn't ready.

It wasn't until years later, through what I learned in the Warrior PATHH Program, that I began to understand something different.

Letting go didn't mean reliving the moment.

It meant understanding how it impacted me.
How it made me feel.

And how I could carry the lesson, without carrying the weight.

I began to release some of those rocks.

Not by staying in the past.

But by learning to reference it, without residing in it.

About a year ago, I read the book *The Mountain Is You.*

There was a quote that stayed with me:

"In order to start a new life, you need to let go of the old one."

That hit me.

Because for more than a decade,

I had been holding on.

Living in the past.

Carrying weight, I didn't know how to release.

But not anymore.

I'm learning to release the shame and guilt I carried from coming home without my brothers who didn't.

By sharing my story, I honor them, living in a way they no longer can, and becoming the version of myself they never had the chance to be.

Because, as Brené Brown reminds us, shame cannot survive being spoken.

Reflection in Song:

Here I Am

When I wake up in the morning
The sunlight on my face
Looking for an adventure
And wondering what it takes.

Looking for the next thing
I want to fight.
Looking for the next thing
I want to get it right.

So here I am
I am waiting for a light
Hoping for an adventure
to manifest insight.

So here I am
I am waiting for a sign
Looking to what's ahead
rather what's left behind

G-C-G-D
(Guitar Chords)

I look at the sky,
as the clouds drift above
And the trees shed their leaves
As they swirl around me.

I listen to the wind
as it blows in my ears
It whispers some lyrics
I needed to hear

So here I am
Don't wait for a light
The adventure you seek
Is all in plain sight

So here I am
Don't wait for a sign
The answers your
looking for
Will be revealed in time

G-C-G-D
(Guitar Chords)

I look in the mirror
and see an old face,
The lines tell the
stories of long-traveled
days.

Then I smile at the
myself,
just to let it be known,
These tales of my life
Are those of my own

So here I am
I'm ready for a fight
On a heroes journey
With nature guides.

So here I am
Letting life unfold,
'Cause this adventure
I'm living, Is a story
worth told

G-C-G-D
(Guitar Chords)

Chapter 8
(The Dragon)

During my early childhood in the 1980s, life felt as normal as it could be.

But as I grew into my teenage years, things began to change.

My father was going through struggles of his own, though at the time, I had no awareness of it. What I did become aware of, was the abuse.

It began with my mother.

And eventually, it extended to us, his children.

For nearly a decade, we lived in fear.

Fear of what might happen next.
Fear of the environment we called home.

We experienced things no child should ever have to witness or endure, physical abuse, whether it came from a belt, a shoe, a metal hanger, or a grown man's fist.

My mother took the brunt of it.

She did everything she could to protect us.

Fear kept her there.
That, and the challenge of navigating life while barely speaking English at the time.

There came a moment, just before I turned 18, when I had reached my limit.

I told my mother that when I turned 18, I was leaving.

I remember my room, it was in the back of the house. I had a gym bag packed and hidden under my bed, waiting for that day.

The day came.

On my 18th birthday, I grabbed my bag and climbed halfway out of the window.

That's when my mom stopped me.

She asked me not to leave.

I told her I had to go.

She asked me for one more week.

Time to prepare herself, and to prepare my younger brother and sister to leave as well.

A week passed.

And I left.

I left my mother.

My brother.

My sister.

I left them behind, with the very thing I was running from.

But not long after, maybe a week or two, they followed.

And that was the last time we ever stepped foot in that house.

Even after leaving, something stayed with me.

Fear.

Anger.

Hate.

As I grew older and joined the military, I realized something: I was still afraid of my father.

I carried so much resentment that I made a decision, his first name would end with me. I chose not to name my firstborn after myself as a symbolic break from him.

From 1994, the year I climbed out that window,

To 2024.

I was still carrying that weight.

But something began to shift.

As I started revisiting my past, with more clarity than I had ever had before, I began remembering things differently.

Not through anger.

But through understanding.

I remembered a moment from childhood.

My father once took us to the place where he had grown up. It was an old, broken-down home.

Behind it stood a tree.

He told us that his mother, our grandmother, used to chase him up that tree with a knife.

At the time, it was just a story.

Now, I see it for what it was:
A disclosure.

As I reflected more, I remembered witnessing that same grandmother abuse her husband when she was drunk.

And that's when something clicked.

My father didn't know what love looked like.

He learned it from the only example he had.

This is not an excuse.

Abuse is not something we inherit like a gene.

It is a choice.

But understanding where it came from, gave me a different perspective.

I made a promise early in my life:

I would never lay a hand on my wife or my children.

What I realized later was this:

I didn't just learn what love was.

I learned what love was not.

And that gave me empathy.

There is nothing I can do to change what happened.

But I can choose how I use it.

Not just to tell a story of survival,

But to remind myself:

I went through all of that,

And I am still here.

That realization gave me something I didn't think I would ever have.

The ability to forgive.

I forgave my father.

Not for him.

But for me.

And in doing so, I began to see something else.

The dragon I feared for so long,

Was guarding something.

A lesson.

A truth.

A form of understanding.

The cave held a treasure.

It showed me what love should never look like.

And because of that,

I was able to create something different.

Today, my siblings and I all raise our children with love, presence, and care.

Before I close this chapter, there's one more moment I want to share.

I was 17 years old.

It was the third time we had left my father.

He found us at an apartment and asked to speak with me.

I got into the car.

He said, "Your mother told me you don't want to come back home."

I said, "No."

He asked, "Why?"

I told him:

"Because you hit us."

He responded by saying he did it to make us stronger.
That the world is tough, and we needed to be tough too.

Then he said something else:

"You're not 18 yet. I can call the police and have you brought
back."

In that moment, two things became clear to me:

He had unknowingly given me my exit plan.

And I didn't agree with his version of strength.

Ironically, when I joined the Army, no Drill Sergeant could
break me in the way my father had already tried.

Through deployments in some of the most difficult
environments, I realized I had developed a level of mental
toughness.

But now, I understand something deeper.

Strength isn't just about what you can endure.

It's about what you choose to become.

Today, I am not the child who feared his father.

I am a man who is not feared by his children.

And in that,

I found peace.

Reflection in Song:

The Gingerbread Man

Runnn
Runnn
Running as fast as I
Can

Runnn
Runnn
Running like
The gingerbread
Man

Jack and Jill and that
One big hill
Mary and her little lambs
In the prairie fields

The three little pigs and
The big bad wolf
Along with little red
Riding hood

These are the stories we were
Told as kids
But no one ever taught us what to do if
The wolf ever wins.

Guitar Solo:
G-D-EM-C-G-C-G-D
(2x)

Runnn
Runnn
Running as fast as I
Can

Runnn
Runnn
Running like
The gingerbread
Man

I close my eyes
Late at night
My soul drifts right into those
Firefights

My dreams go to sleep
Inside of me
Allowing that big bad wolf to
Chase and run free

I ran my whole life like
The gingerbread man
Never looking back, to
Where my story began.

Runnn
Runnn
Running as fast as I
Can

Runnn
Runnn
Running like
The gingerbread
Man

Guitar Solo:
G-D-EM-C-G-C-G-D
(2x)

I don't want a destiny to be
Written for me.
No ceilings. No walls.
Or victim to see

I want to be the best version
Of me
Living a best life that I know
I can be

Runnn
Runnn
Running as fast as I
Can

Runnn
Runnn
Running like
The gingerbread
Man

But maybe running taught me
How to last
How to carry the weight
How to move through the past.

I don't have to win every
Race I can
Sometimes strength is knowing
When to stand.

Like Jack on the bean stalk or
With the candle stick
Or the tortoise who beat the hare
That was really quick

I ran to survive.
I stopped to grow
Now I walk forward
And I finally know.

Runnn
Runnn
Running as fast as I
Can

Runnn
Runnn
Running like
The gingerbread
Man

Runnn
Runnn
I'm running as fast as I
Can

Runnn
Runnn
Well, I'm the Gingerbread
Man

Guitar Solo:
G-D-EM-C-G-C-G-D
(2x)

Chords: Em-C-G-D

Chapter 9
(The Elixir)

As I found grace and forgiveness over the past year, I began to reflect on how far I had truly come.

This wasn't just about telling a story anymore.

It was about answering a question I could no longer avoid:

Was I simply teaching Post-Traumatic Growth,
or was I actually living it?

I began to challenge myself.

What happens when life tests me again?
What happens when my belief system is pushed to its limits?

Would I fall back into old habits?
Would I label the moment as failure or would I see it as an opportunity for growth?

And then,

It happened.

The ground beneath me shifted.

The cave rumbled.

The mountain I stood near the exit of the cave. Everything I thought was stable, moved.

Another step into the unknown.

But this time.

Something was different.

Instead of resisting it.

I welcomed it.

I remember sitting there, almost in conversation with myself.

"Alright, here we go again."

A pause.

Then another voice, stronger this time:

"No blame. No victim. No villain. Just the next chapter."

For the first time, I felt like I had the pen in my hand.

Life wasn't writing the story for me anymore.

I was.

When I walked out the door of Warrior PATHH in April of 2022, life came at me fast.

It felt like I was a young warrior, just stepping onto the battlefield, learning as I went, barely dodging what came my way.

But now?

Now I felt ready.

Grounded.

Aware.

I remember thinking:

"I've been here before, but not like this."

This time, I wasn't reacting, I was responding.

Fully armored, not in defense, but in understanding.

Ready to step into who I was meant to be.

On 28 July 2022, I made the decision to move on from the position I had held for the past two years and step into the unknown once again.

As I entered the unknown, two thoughts stayed with me:

Finish your master's program.

Start something of your own.

And just like that, my mindset shifted.

From:

"What if this doesn't work?"

To:

"What now?"

I actually said it out loud one day.

"What now?"

And I smiled.

Because it didn't feel like fear anymore.

It felt like a possibility.

There was no need to sit in what had already happened.

No need to replay it.

No need to stay there.

Because the question wasn't "why."

It was:

What now?

That became my theme.

At first, I had an idea.

I wanted to start a tourism company called What Now?

The concept was simple, creating experiences for people; show them the beauty of the city and its lakes, giving them something memorable.

But as I started digging into it, running numbers, thinking through logistics, I felt something inside me pause.

"This isn't it."

So, I did something different.

I asked for help.

I connected with a career consultant and joined a Zoom call with a group of entrepreneurs.

After hearing a bit of my story, the career consultant reached out.

"Hey," he said, "I'd like to offer you a one-on-one session. No cost. Just a conversation."

I agreed.

That one hour changed everything.

He asked me some simple questions.

"What did you enjoy most about your previous roles?"
"When did you feel most fulfilled?"
"What made you smile?"

I paused.

Thought about it.

Then I answered honestly.

And somewhere in that conversation.

It hit me.

Not something he said.

Not something he suggested.

Something I realized.

I leaned back, looked at the screen, and said it out loud:

"I think I know what I want to do."

He smiled.

"What is it?"

I took a breath.

"I want to be a life coach."

In that moment, it felt like lightning.

Not loud.

Not overwhelming.

Clear.

Like something that had always been there was finally being acknowledged.

My calling.

As the call ended, I sat there for a moment.

Quiet.

Letting it sink in.

Then another thought came to me:

What is the name of this company?

And almost instantly, I remembered.

A few years earlier, I was sitting at lunch with a group of friends.

We were talking and sharing ideas.

I remember mention a phrase:

"Strive To Thrive."

How this would be a great name for a company.

One of my friends nodded and said,

"That would be a good name."

At the time, it was just a moment.

A thought.

A passing idea.

But now,

It was something more.

It was real.

On September 7, 2025,
Strive To Thrive LLC: A Self-Care Journey was born.

And in that moment, everything connected.

My past.
My experiences.
My struggles.
My growth.

They weren't random.

They weren't wasted.

They were preparing me.

I wasn't just moving forward anymore.

I was moving with purpose.

And yet,

It didn't feel like an ending.

It felt like a beginning.

Reflection in Song:

The Calling

Walking down the path
One day at a time
Looking for a day
That I can call mine

Where my story
Will end or go
Will depend on my calling
I feel in my soul

Waiting for that moment
That puts a spark in my eye
Becoming a superhero
Fly high

Whooh!
I ready to roar
Waiting for my calling
So, I can sour

Whooh!
I ready to soar
Waiting for my calling
So, I can roar

G-D-Em-C
(Guitar Chords)

The days roll on
The hours slide
The sands of time
Just pass me by

I watch the birds
Across the sky
One grain of life
One breath at a time

I'll live in the present
My calling will know
Where I'm headed
Or where to go.

Whooh!
I ready to roar
Waiting for my calling
So, I can sour

Whooh!
I ready to soar
Waiting for my calling
So, I can roar

I used to fear
The unknown road
Every shadow,
Every load

But now I see
The light in me
The strength to choose
Who I will be

D-Em-C-G

The day it called
It knocked on my door
Didn't tell me
What it had in stored

It only said,
"Here's a seed,"
"It's up to you
What it will be."

G-D-Em-C
(Guitar Chords)

Whooh!
I ready to roar
Waiting for my calling
So, I can sour

Whooh!
I ready to soar
Waiting for my calling
So, I can roar

Waiting for my calling
So, I can roar

Walking down this path
One day at a time
I finally found my calling
That I can call mine

Chapter 10
(A New Beginning: Living My Calling)

If you had asked me 4 years ago where I would be today, I don't think I could have answered you.

Not because I didn't have goals.

But because I didn't yet have clarity.

Today, I stand in a different place.

Not a place of perfection,

But a place of awareness.

The journey I've shared in this book didn't end when I walked out of the program.

It didn't end when I left my job.

It didn't end when I faced the caves I had avoided for years.

It continues.

Every single day.

Because what I've learned is this:

Post-Traumatic Growth is not a moment.

It's a lifestyle.

Today, I live that lifestyle through service.

Through connection.

Through presence.

I show up.

I show up in my coaching, helping others navigate their own journeys, not by telling them what to do, but by walking alongside them as they discover it for themselves.

I show up in my live sessions, night after night, creating a space where people can come as they are, be heard, and be seen.

I show up through music, writing, and expressing the parts of life that words alone sometimes cannot capture.

I show up in my education, completing my academic goals, not just for achievement, but for growth.

I show up through creation, writing books, sharing stories, and building something that didn't exist before I chose to begin.

And I show up through Strive To Thrive LLC, a vision that was once just a thought, now becoming something real.

None of this came from having all the answers.

It came from asking better questions.

From:

"Why is this happening to me?"

To:

"What is this trying to teach me?"

From:

"What if I fail?"

To:

"What now?"

There was a time in my life when I believed strength meant enduring everything,

Carrying it all,

Holding it in.

Now I understand something different:

Strength is not just what you carry.

It's what you choose to release.

There was a time when I believed I had to control everything,

People, outcomes, and situations.

Now I see it clearly:

Growth happens through connection,
Not control.

There was also a time when I believed my past defined me.

Now I know:

It prepared me.

Every storm.
Every cave.

Every moment I wanted to quit,
Every moment I didn't understand.

They weren't working against me.

They were shaping me.

And if there is one thing I hope you take from this book, it's
this:

You are not broken.
You are becoming.

Whatever you've been through,
Whatever you're facing right now.

There is something on the other side of it.

Not because it disappears,
But because you grow through it.

This isn't the end.

It's a new beginning.

I'm no longer waiting for purpose to find me.

I've chosen to live it.

Everything I've experienced has led me here.

Not to keep me in the past, but to move me forward with clarity, strength, and intention.

Today, I live my calling.

And I will continue to show up, serve, and grow, one step at a time.

Because the journey doesn't end here.

It begins again.

Reflection in Song:

Struggle To Strength

I grew up in stormy weathers
Lightning crashing every night
The unknown knowledge to thrive
A seed not in my life

The only thing I knew
Was to run and close my eyes
Hoping for a wishing star
To saving me every night

So those days I knew
They wouldn't last
As I grew up through the years
And forgot my past

And these days I knew
They would go fast
As the sand of that time
Turn into Ash

G-D-Em-C
(Guitar Chords)

Now I'm looking back
To where I use to be
That Cave that I feared
Holds them treasures I seek

Looking for that light
In the pitch of the dark
Searching for that elixir
That puts sparks in my heart

So those days I knew
They wouldn't last
As I grew up through the years
And forgot my past

And these days I knew
They would go fast
As the sand of that time
Turn into Ash

As I'm running through the cave
Within inside of me,
I hear a voice whisper
Come this way and see

I find a path
To where I am
To begin a new life
from where I stand

Em-D-C-G
(Guitar Chords)

So those days I knew
They wouldn't last
As I grew up through the years
And forgot my past

And these days I knew
They would go fast
As the sand of that time
Turn into Ash

G-D-Em-C
(Guitar Chords)

That voice that whispered
Inside my ear
Is the same old voice
That has always been here

A phoenix is born
From all of this ash
As it shoots up to the sky
With a golden flash

So, it's up to me
To give myself grace
In this hero's journey
Called Struggle to Strength

So, it's up to me
To give myself grace
In this hero's journey
Called Struggle to Strength

Reflection in Songs

There were moments in this journey where words alone weren't enough.

Where thoughts turned into feelings, and feelings needed a different way to be expressed.

Music became that space.

These songs are not separate from the story you've just read; they are an extension of it.

They were written in the quiet moments, the reflective moments, and the moments I was still trying to understand what I was feeling.

Some were written in the middle of the storm.

Others came after, when I could finally see clearly.

Each lyric holds a piece of the journey, of struggle, growth, awareness, and purpose.

If the chapters spoke to your mind, my hope is that these songs speak to your heart.

Waiting For A Light

I'm sitting here
In the dark
Waiting for a light,
Or a shooting star

Well, I'm sitting in the dark
Waiting for a light up
Waiting for a shooting star to
Light up the night

When I was young
The days where cold
The winds of change
Blew through my soul.

Everywhere
I looked around
All I saw were
Shadows on the walls

So, I grab my bags
And left on a trail
Never looking back to
See what's there.

I'm sitting here
In the dark
Waiting for a light,
Or a shooting star

Well, I'm sitting in the dark
Waiting for a light up
Waiting for a shooting star to
Light up the night

I said
Heyy Yoo!
Heyy
Let the four winds blow

And I said,
Heyy Yoo!
Waiting for that
Heavenly glow

————

As the years have passed
The days are cold
The winds of change
Keep blowing through my soul.

Whren a door appears
Around some trees,
I'm walking in a labyrinth
With a warm cool breeze.

Then, I grab a rock from my
Heart of within
And I throw it in fire so
My life could begin

Well, I'm still sitting
In the dark
Waiting for a light,
Or a shooting star

I said
Heyy Yoo!
Heyy
Let the four winds blow

And I said,
Heyy Yoo!
Waiting for that
Heavenly glow

————

Now the winds of change
Begins to soar
My Gratitude for life runs
Through my soul

Now I'm looking back
from where I came
I get to write my story without
Any shame

Then I stand right up
With my head up high
As shower of shooting stars
Light up the sky

Well, I'm not sitting in the dark
Waiting for a light
Or waiting for a shooting star
light up the night.

No, I'm now standing up
With my head up high
As a shower of shooting stars
light up the sky.

I said
Heyy Yoo!
Heyy
Let the four winds blow

And I said,
Heyy Yoo!
Watching that
Heavenly glow

G-C-G-D
(Guitar Chords)

Struggle To Strength

I grew up in stormy weathers
Lightning crashing every night
The unknown knowledge to thrive
A seed not in my life

The only thing I knew
Was to run and close my eyes
Hoping for a wishing star
To saving me every night

So those days I knew
They wouldn't last
As I grew up through the years
And forgot my past

And these days I knew
They would go fast
As the sand of that time
Turn into Ash

G-D-Em-C
(Guitar Chords)

Now I'm looking back
To where I use to be
That Cave that I feared
Holds them treasures I seek

Looking for that light
In the pitch of the dark
Searching for that elixir
That puts sparks in my heart

So those days I knew
They wouldn't last
As I grew up through the years
And forgot my past

And these days I knew
They would go fast
As the sand of that time
Turn into Ash

As I'm running through the cave
Within inside of me,
I hear a voice whisper
Come this way and see

I find a path
to where I am
To begin a new life
from where I stand

Em-D-C-G
(Guitar Chords)

So those days I knew
They wouldn't last
As I grew up through the years
And forgot my past

And these days I knew
They would go fast
As the sand of that time
Turn into Ash

G-D-Em-C
(Guitar Chords)

That voice that whispered
inside my ear
is the same old voice
That has always been here

A phoenix is born
from all of this ash
As it shoots up to the sky
with a golden flash

So, it's up to me
To give myself grace
In this hero's journey
Called Struggle to Strength

So, it's up to me
To give myself grace
In this hero's journey
Called Struggle to Strength

The Calling

Walking down the path
One day at a time
Looking for a day
That I can call mine

Where my story
Will end or go
Will depend on my calling
I feel in my soul

Waiting for that moment
That puts a spark in my eye
Becoming a superhero
Fly high

Whooh!
I ready to roar
Waiting for my calling
So, I can sour

Whooh!
I ready to soar
Waiting for my calling
So, I can roar

G-D-Em-C
(Guitar Chords)

The days roll on
The hours slide
The sands of time
Just pass me by

I watch the birds
Across the sky
One grain of life
One breath at a time

I'll live in the present
My calling will know
Where I'm headed
Or where to go.

Whooh!
I ready to roar
Waiting for my calling
So, I can sour

Whooh!
I ready to soar
Waiting for my calling
So, I can roar

I used to fear
The unknown road
Every shadow,
every load

But now I see
The light in me
The strength to choose
who I will be

D-Em-C-G
(Guitar Chords)

The day it called
It knocked on my door
Didn't tell me
What it had in stored

It only said,
"Here's a seed,"
"It's up to you
What it will be."

G-D-Em-C
(Guitar Chords)

Whooh!
I ready to roar
Waiting for my calling
So, I can sour

Whooh!
I ready to soar
Waiting for my calling
So, I can roar

Waiting for my calling
So, I can roar

Walking down this path
One day at a time
I finally found my calling
That I can call mine

Here I Am

When I wake up in the morning
The sunlight on my face
Looking for an adventure
And wondering what it takes.

Looking for the next thing
I want to fight.
Looking for the next thing
I want to get it right.

So here I am
I am waiting for a light
Hoping for an adventure
to manifest insight.

So here I am
I am waiting for a sign
Looking to what's ahead
rather what's left behind

G-C-G-D
(Guitar Chords)

I look at the sky,
As the clouds drift above
And the trees shed their leaves
As they swirl around me.

I listen to the wind
As it blows in my ears
It whispers some lyrics
I needed to hear

So here I am
Don't wait for a light
The adventure you seek
Is all in plain sight

So here I am
Don't wait for a sign
The answers your looking for
Will be revealed in time

G-C-G-D
(Guitar Chords)

I look in the mirror
and see an old face,
The lines tell the
stories of long-traveled days.

Then I smile at the myself,
Just to let it be known,
These tales of my life
Are those of my own

So here I am
I'm ready for a fight
On a heroes journey
With nature guides.

So here I am
Letting life unfold,
'Cause this adventure
I'm living, Is a story worth told

G-C-G-D
(Guitar Chords)

The Gingerbread Man

Runnn
Runnn
Running as fast as I
Can

Runnn
Runnn
Running like
The gingerbread
Man

Jack and Jill and that
One big hill
Mary and her little lambs
In the prairie fields

The three little pigs and
The big bad wolf
Along with little red
Riding hood

These are the stories we were
Told as kids
But no one ever taught us what to do if
The wolf ever wins.

Guitar Solo:
G-D-EM-C-G-C-G-D
(2x)

Runnn
Runnn
Running as fast as I
Can

Runnn
Runnn
Running like
The gingerbread
Man

I close my eyes
Late at night
My soul drifts right into those
Firefights

My dreams go to sleep
Inside of me
Allowing that big bad wolf to
Chase and run free

I ran my whole life like
The gingerbread man
Never looking back, to
Where my story began.

Runnn
Runnn
Running as fast as I
Can

Runnn
Runnn
Running like
The gingerbread
Man

Guitar Solo:
G-D-EM-C-G-C-G-D
(2x)

I don't want a destiny to be
written for me.
No ceilings. No walls.
Or victim to see

I want to be the best version
of me
Living a best life that I know
I can be

Runnn
Runnn
Running as fast as I
Can

Runnn
Runnn
Running like
The gingerbread
Man

But maybe running taught me
How to last
How to carry the weight
How to move through the past.

I don't have to win every
Race I can
Sometimes strength is knowing
When to stand.

Like Jack on the bean stalk or
With the candle stick
Or the tortoise who beat the hare
That was really quick

I ran to survive.
I stopped to grow
Now I walk forward
and I finally know.

Runnn
Runnn
Running as fast as I
Can

Runnn
Runnn
Running like
The gingerbread
Man

Runnn
Runnn
I'm running as fast as I
Can

Runnn
Runnn
Well, I'm the Gingerbread
Man

Guitar Solo:
G-D-EM-C-G-C-G-D
(2x)

Main Guitar Chords: Em-C-G-D

Acknowledgments & Influences

This journey is deeply personal, shaped by experience, reflection, and growth over time.

I want to acknowledge Billy Britt, whose words helped shift my perspective at a time I didn't realize I needed it. That moment, what I often describe as "my glass shattering" became the beginning of a new path forward.

I also want to recognize Lamont Christian, a mentor who reached out early in my journey and introduced me to opportunities that planted seeds of curiosity and growth.

I'm grateful for Melenie Stewart, who has become both a trusted companion and a great friend. As we continue to grow our own companies, her presence, perspective, and support have meant a great deal in my journey.

The concept of Post-Traumatic Growth, developed by Richard Tedeschi and Lawrence Calhoun, has been instrumental in shaping my understanding of growth through adversity. Insights from The Mountain Is You also influenced my perspective on letting go and moving forward.

I am grateful for The Big Red Barn Retreat, The Warrior PATHH Program and the community of veterans, first responders, mentors, and peers who have supported me along the way.

Growth is not something we achieve alone, it is shaped through connection, shared experience, and the willingness to keep learning.

The Hero's Journey: An Overview

The Hero's Journey is a framework introduced by Joseph Campbell that describes a common pattern found in stories, myths, and personal transformation. It outlines the stages individuals often move through when facing change, challenge, and growth.

While it is often used in storytelling, it also reflects real-life experiences of transition, struggle, and becoming.

The Stages of the Hero's Journey

1. The Ordinary World:
This is where the journey begins, in the familiar. Life feels structured, predictable, and known.

2. The Call to Adventure:
A challenge, opportunity, or realization appears, inviting the individual into something new or uncertain.

3. Refusal of the Call:
Hesitation or resistance may occur. Fear, doubt, or uncertainty can make stepping forward feel difficult.

4. Meeting the Mentor:
Guidance appears through a person, experience, or insight that provides support, encouragement, or direction.

5. Crossing the Threshold:
A decision is made to move forward. This marks the transition from the known into the unknown.

6. Tests, Allies, and Challenges:
Along the journey, obstacles arise. Relationships form,
lessons are learned, and growth begins to take shape.

7. Approach to the Inner Cave:
The journey turns inward. This stage involves preparing to
face deeper fears, truths, or unresolved experiences.

8. The Ordeal:
A significant challenge or turning point occurs. This is often
the most difficult moment of the journey, where
transformation is possible.

9. The Reward (The Elixir):
After facing the challenge, insight, clarity, or growth is gained.
A new understanding begins to emerge.

10. The Road Back:
The individual begins to integrate what they have learned and
prepares to return to their life with a new perspective.

11. The Resurrection:
A final test or moment of reflection reinforces the
transformation. Old patterns are replaced with new ways of
being.

12. The Return with the Gift:
The journey comes full circle. The individual returns not as
who they were, but as who they have become—bringing their
growth, insight, and experience forward.

About the Author

Daniel Navarro is a U.S. Army veteran whose military journey spans 23 years, including multiple deployments to the Middle East. Throughout his service, he led, mentored, and coached others in high-performance environments, developing individuals and teams to grow through challenge and adversity.

After transitioning out of the military, Daniel faced the challenges of identity, purpose, and direction that many experience when stepping into the unknown. Through his journey, he discovered the power of Post-Traumatic Growth, a mindset that transforms adversity into opportunity.

Daniel is the founder of **Strive To Thrive LLC**, a life coaching and personal development company focused on helping individuals grow through life's challenges, build self-awareness, and live with intention and purpose.

He hosts live sessions, facilitates group conversations, and creates content centered on mental wellness, growth, and connection. He is also a writer, speaker, and musician who believes in the power of storytelling to inspire transformation.

His mission is simple:

To sharing the knowledge, he has learned with other.

Emphasizing his quote:

"A seed of knowledge will branch out to help many"